S for Sengoku

ISBN: 979-8-8693-6472-2

Introduction

The Sengoku Period of Feudal Japan was a very

influential part of world history.

Various states declared war on each other,

which lasted 184 years.

In comparison, the American Civil War only

lasted 4 years.

Foreign influences, such as the Catholic Church

and the Portuguese, also played a role in

supporting different sides of the war.

This book will detail the factions and events

that impacted Japan, both militarily and

societally.

Regions

Japan can be divided into 4 islands.

More specifically, Hokkaido, Shikoku, Kyushu,

and Honshu.

Japan can also be divided into 8 regions.

More specifically, Hokkaido, Tohoku, Kanto,

Chubu, Kansai, Chugoku, Shikoku, and

Kyushu.

Various Samurai clans controlled different

regions and even certain states or prefectures of

a region.

Some Samurai Clans controlled an entire island

during the Sengoku period.

Hokkaido

Hokkaido is the northernmost island of Japan and is its own state.

It is similar to the state of Alaska as it is a predominately frozen wasteland with little to no benefit for a military or civilian population in terms of resources and land.

As a result, the island of Hokkaido was virtually untouched and had virtually no warfare take place on it during the course of the Sengoku Period.

Tohoku

Tohoku is in the northernmost region of Honshu.

It is divided into the states (now called prefectures) of Aomori, Akita, Iwate, Yamagata, Miyagi and Fukushima.

In terms of climate, culture, and geography, it is similar to that of the East Coast of the United States.

Tohoku had a lot of wars between clans take place during the Sengoku Period since most of the war was fought on the island of Honshu.

Kanto

Kanto is in the southeasternmost region of

Honshu.

It is divided into the states (now called

prefectures) of Tochigi, Ibaraki, Chiba,

Saitama, Gunma, Kanagawa, and Tokyo.

In terms of climate and geography, it is similar

to that of the New York, since it is where a

large chunk of the population is located.

Kanto had a lot of wars between clans take

place during the Sengoku Period since most of

the war was fought on the island of Honshu.

Chubu

Chubu is in the central region of Honshu.

It is divided into the states (now called

prefectures) of Nigata, Toyama, Ishikawa

Fukui, Gifu, Nagano, Yamanashi, Achi, and

Shizuoka.

In terms of climate, culture, and geography it is

similar to that of the New England of the

United States.

Chubu had a lot of wars between clans take

place during the Sengoku Period since most of

the war was fought on the island of Honshu.

Kansai

Kansai is in the southernmost region of Honshu.

It is divided into the states (now called prefectures) of Kyoto, Hyogo, Shiga, Mie, Nara, Osaka, and Wakayama.

In terms of climate, culture, and geography, it is similar to that of the Southern United States since it is coastal and can be humid.

Kansai had a lot of wars between clans take place during the Sengoku Period since most of the war was fought on the island of Honshu.

Chugoku

Chugoku is in the western most region of Honshu.

It is divided into the states (now called prefectures) of Tottori, Okayama, Hiroshima, Yamaguchi, and Shimane.

In terms of climate, culture, and geography, it is similar to that of the Midwest United States.

Chugoku had a lot of wars between clans take place during the Sengoku Period since most of the war was fought on the island of Honshu.

Shikoku

Shikoku is south central island of Japan.

It is divided into the states (now called prefectures) of Kagawa, Ehime, Tokushima, and Kochi.

In terms of climate and geography, it is similar to that of the Rocky Mountains of the United States.

Shikoku had a lot of wars between clans take place during the Sengoku Period since it was invaded by clans from Honshu.

Kyushu

Kyushu is the southernmost island of Japan.

It is divided into the states (now called prefectures) of Okinawa, Fukouka, Saga, Oita, Miyazaki, Nagasaki, Kumamoto, Okinawa and Kagoshima.

In terms of climate and geography, it is similar to that of the West Coast of the United States.

Kyushu had a lot of wars between clans take place during the Sengoku period since it was invaded by clans from Honshu.

Society

The society of Japan during the Sengoku Period was based on a feudal system.

It primarily had nobility at the top of the societal pyramid in Japan, who were essentially figureheads.

The next level in the middle of this societal pyramid was military leaders and warriors, who kept the people in line.

The lowest level at the bottom of the pyramid were the common folk that made up society as farmers, merchants and artisans.

Emperor

The Emperor was the ruler of Japan.

They were essentially a figurehead that led the

country of Japan.

It was similar to the King of England in terms

of power and authority.

The Emperor was more of a ceremonial

position rather than one of actual legal or

military authority.

Kuge

Kuge were court nobility in Japan.

They were a civil aristocracy in Japan that helped with decision-making and advised on certain policies.

It was similar to the Royal Family of England with regards to influence and ability to sway public opinion regarding the war.

Shogun

The Shogun was the de facto ruler of Japan.

It was a title of administration and military

leadership in Japan.

They were similar to the Prime Minster of

England or President of the United States with

regards to power and authority.

They were also Commander in Chief of all the

Daimyo in Japan.

Without a shogun, there was no clear leader to

take orders from in each state or region of

Japan.

Daimyo

The Daimyo were samurai feudal lords.

They were high ranking samurai and ruled individual states of Japan.

They were similar to governors of state in America.

They each controlled a different state or region of Japan.

Some Daimyos formed alliances between states to control a region of Japan, such as the Kanto region.

Retainers

Retainers were samurai that served a daimyo.

They provided military service and loyalty in exchange for protection, land, and other benefits.

They were similar to military officers in Japan.

While they were not bound by oath to serve a Daimyo, they were essentially bound by obligation due to receiving some sort of good or service in exchange for their advice and military skills.

Vassals

Vassals were essentially loyal subjects that served the Shogun.

It was similar to a cabinet secretary in the United States.

They helped provide advice on military strategy in order to win battles.

They also advised on domestic policy with regards to how the state should function and keep the population under control.

Samurai

Samurai were a novel warrior class in Feudal Japan.

They reported to a Daimyo in a clan or state they were based in.

They were similar to military soldier in Japan.

The relationship was similar to being a full-time employee at a job, although this was more of a military or security role.

Ronin

Ronin were samurai without a master.

They did not report to a daimyo, which made their loyalty very fluid.

They were similar to mercenaries for hire.

This was similar tot a freelance contractor for a company, or in this case, a sword or gun for hire.

Due to their lack of allegiance or loyalty to a specific clan, they could easily join a different clan against one of their previous clans if the price was right.

Komuso

Komuso were wandering lay Buddhists that
journeyed across Japan.

They were known for wearing straw basket hats
and playing bamboo flutes.

They acted as spies that hid in plain sight since
you could not see their faces through their hats.

They would help the war effort by providing
lodging to ronin and samurai on behalf of the
daimyo and their government.

Sumo

Sumo were combat trainers for the warriors in samurai Clans.

They also acted as bodyguards for samurai and daimyo.

Due to their large size and intimidating looks, many people would not dare to approach these people.

Sumo would eventually evolve into a sport that is till recognized and participated in to this very day.

Yabusame

Yabusame were Japanese cavalry.

They also acted as archers and helped assist the

Ashigaru in battle.

The horses they had used to ride on were

brought overseas by the Portuguese.

The Yabusame helped reinforce the armies on

the front lines and were also used in raids

against other clans.

Kyudo

Kyudo were Japanese archers.

They helped perform assassinations from far away, similar to modern-day snipers.

The bows and arrows they used were domestic and from Japan.

These types of soldiers were different from others, as they used Japanese-made weaponry to fight for their clan.

Ashigaru

Ashigaru were foot soldiers of Japan.

They were essentially front line infantry for

Samurai clans.

They were known for using matchlock guns and

other European weapons that were brought to

Japan by the Portuguese.

Due to European involvement, the warfare of

Japan became even more deadly due to the

introduction of firearms into Japanese clan

arsenals.

Shinobi

Shinobi were spies that worked for a daimyo.

They performed reconnaissance, espionage, sabotage, and assassinations.

Male Shinobi were called Ninjas.

Female Shinobi were called Kunoichi.

They were similar to FBI or CIA agents in Japan.

Some had allegiance to certain clans, while others were without a master and could easily change sides if they wanted to.

Peasants

Peasants were the farming class of Japan.

They were mainly in rural areas and helped support society by growing food.

Some peasants started revolts against their daimyo if their living conditions were worse during the war.

A large portion of the population of Japan was peasantry, since Japan was primarily an agrarian society during the Sengoku Period.

Artisans

Artisans were a good producing class of Japan.

They were mainly in urban areas and helped

support society by producing goods.

They helped create tools for the common folk

to use, as well as weapons for the military to

use in combat.

Not many people in Japan were artisans at the

time, so their skills in craftsman ship were

essential for the war effort as well as domestic

production.

Merchants

Merchants were the businessmen and sellers of goods and services in Japan.

They were also in an urban area that helped support society by selling goods and food to people in Japan.

This helped the local economies of the states.

Due to the war, there was not a lot of interstate commerce, so many merchants could only sell their goods in the state or region that they were in.

Machibugyo

Machibugyo were samurai that acted as local city administrators or commissioners in a town or village.

They acted as Chief of Police, prosecutors, judges and other criminal justice officials in cities and towns.

They kept the peace and made sure that criminals were held accountable.

They also tried to mitigate the risk of rebellions and uprisings from occurring in towns and villages.

Yoriki

Yoriki were samurai police officers.

They managed patrols and guard units.

They helped keep the peace by being the eyes and ears of the daimyo as well as other local law enforcement officials in the town or village they were in.

They also helped manage the prison population in their jurisdiction.

Doshin

Doshin were samurai security guards.

They investigated crimes, helped guard prisoners, and carried out executions.

They wore multiple hats for the local samurai police force.

As a result, they had a lot of responsibilities to keep the peace and assist different levels of society.

Komono

Komono were non-samurai common folk.

They provided assistance to Doshin on patrols,

similar to a records technician or evidence

technician.

As a result, they were civilian police assistants

that helped do administrative task and other

unarmed work for samurai police forces in

towns.

Okappiki

Okappiki were former criminals who helped the samurai police.

They worked for the Doshin as informants and spies.

Due to their connections to the criminal underground in feudal Japan, they were a valuable asset in finding traitors, spies, rebels, and other people that threatened the stability of society.

Factions

Various factions were involved in the Sengoku Period.

There were 4 major alliances across the Sengoku Period.

These include the Honganji Rioters, the Saika Renegades, the Western Army, and the Eastern Army.

These can be divided into 20 Prominent Clans across different periods of the Sengoku Period

More specifically, the Ashikaga, Hosokawa, Miyoshi, Tokugawa, Toyotomi, Oda, Takeda, Uesugi, Hojo, Mori, Imagawa, Saito, Date

Shimazu, Chosokabe, Azai, Akechi, Sanada, Kuroda, and Tachibana Clans.

The first 80 years were a series of unorganized uprisings across Japan that mainly involved the Three Dividers.

More specifically, Yoshihisa Ashikaga, Katsumoto Hosokawa, and Nagayoshi Miyoshi.

The last 50 years of the war were primarily controlled by the Three Unifiers.

More specifically, Nobunaga Oda, Hideyoshi, Toyotomi, and Ieyasu Tokugawa.

The Catholic Church and Portuguese also

played a role in supporting the war among

different factions.

Honganji Rioters

The Honganji Rioters were a a group of monks

and peasants who opposed Nobunaga Oda on

religious grounds.

With over 500,000 members, they posed a great

threa to the Oda Clan.

The Honganji would eventually form an

alliance with the Saika Renegades to oppose

imperial samurai rule in general, which was

taking place in Japan.

Saika Renegades

The Saika Renegades were insurgents who opposed imperial samurai authority.

They were mainly composed of sailors, pirates, traders, and other mercenaries.

They were led by Mahoichi Saika, and their army and navy were as strong as 5,000 troops.

They were also allies of the Honganji Rioters due to their mutual distrust and hostility toward samurai warlords.

Western Army

The Western Army was an alliance created to defend Toyotomi reign after Hideyoshi Toyotomi's death after he unified Japan.

It had over 125,000 members and was led by Hideyori Toyotomi, Hideyoshi's son.

It was similar to the Union during the American Civil War.

The Western Army faced multiple battles against the Eastern Army near the end of the Sengoku Period.

Eastern Army

The Eastern Army was an alliance that opposed

Toyotomi reign after Hideyoshi Toyotomi's

death after he unified Japan.

It had over 85,000 members and was led by

Ieyasu Tokugawa.

It was similar to the Confederacy in the

American Civil War.

The Eastern Army faced multiple battles

against the Western Army near the end of the

Sengoku Period.

Catholic Church

The Catholic Church was involved in the Sengoku Period just before the Three Unifiers phase.

They helped bring food, shelter, and missionary work to evangelize the Japanese population.

The Tokugawa Shogunate would persecute European and Japanese Christians after Christianity was outlawed near the end of the Sengoku Period.

The Portuguese

The Portuguese were involved in the Sengoku period around the same time as the Catholic Church.

They provided weapons, ammunition, horses and mercantile trade to Japan.

They tried to colonize Japan and took advantage of the civil war that divided the population.

Their failed colonization of Japan led to them being expelled from Japan by the Tokugawa Shogunate.

Ashikaga Clan

The Ashikaga Clan was a samurai clan during

the Sengoku Period.

It was led by Yoshihisa Ashikaga.

They were primarily based in the Tochigi

Prefecture in the Kanto Region on the island of

Honshu in Japan.

They ruled until 1573 as the Shogunate of

Japan until they were deposed by Nobunaga

Oda.

They were one of the Three Dividers during the

first half of the Sengoku Period.

Hosokawa Clan

The Hosokawa Clan was a samurai clan during the Sengoku Period.

It was led by Katsumoto Hosokawa.

They were primarily based on the island of Honshu, but they also controlled the islands of Kyushu and Shikoku for many periods.

They ruled were known for being involved in the Onin War and were one of the Three Dividers that tore Japan apart during the first half of the Sengoku Period.

Miyoshi Clan

The Miyoshi Clan was a samurai clan during

the Sengoku Period.

It was led by Yoshinaga Miyoshi.

They were primarily based in the Kansai

Region on the island of Honshu and were also

in Tokushima on the island of Shikoku

They ruled until 1582 when they officially

dissolved as a clan.

They were one of the Three Dividers during the

first half of the Sengoku Period.

Tokugawa Clan

The Tokugawa Clan was a samurai clan during

the Sengoku Period.

It was led by Ieyasu Tokugawa.

They were primarily based in Aichi in the

Chubu region on the island of Honshu in Japan.

They ruled until 1867 when the Shogunate was

formally abolished.

They were one of the Three unifiers during the

second half of the Sengoku Period.

Toyotomi Clan

The Toyotomi Clan was a samurai clan during

the Sengoku Period.

It was led by Hideyoshi Toyotomi.

They were not primarily based in a specific

state or region on the island of Honshu in

Japan.

They ruled until 1615 after the Siege of Osaka

Castle.

They were one of the Three unifiers during the

second half of the Sengoku Period.

Oda Clan

The Oda Clan was a samurai clan during the Sengoku Period.

It was led by Nobunaga Oda.

They were primarily based in the Aichi and Fukui states in the Chubu region on the island of Honshu in Japan.

They ruled until 1871 after the abolition of the han system.

They were one of the Three unifiers during the second half of the Sengoku Period.

Takeda Clan

The Takeda Clan was a samurai clan during the Sengoku Period.

It was led by Shingen Takeda.

They were primarily based in the Yamanashi state in the Chubu region on the island of Honshu in Japan.

They ruled until 1582 after they were defeated by Nobunaga Oda.

They were rivals of the Uesugi Clan.

Uesugi Clan

The Uesugi Clan was a samurai clan during the Sengoku Period.

It was led by Kenshin Uesugi.

They were primarily based in the Hyogo, Nigata, Yamagata, and Akita states in the Chubu and Tohoku regions on the island of Honshu in Japan.

They ruled until 1868 after the abolition of the han system.

They were rivals with the Takeda Clan.

Hojo Clan

The Hojo Clan was a samurai clan during the

Sengoku Period.

It was led by Ujiyasu Hojo.

They were primarily based in the Shizuoka and

Kanagawa states in the Chubu and Kanto

regions on the island of Honshu in Japan.

They ruled until 1591 after the Siege of

Odawara.

They were allies of the Imagawa Clan and

Takeda Clan.

Mori Clan

The Mori Clan was a samurai clan during the Sengoku Period.

It was led by Motonari Mori.

They were primarily based in the Kanagawa and Hiroshima states in the Kanto and Chugoku regions on the island of Honshu in Japan.

They ruled until 1868 after the Boshin War and during the Meiji Restoration.

They were allies of the Toyotomi Clan and Tokugawa Clan.

Imagawa Clan

The Imagawa Clan was a samurai clan during

the Sengoku Period.

It was led by Yoshimoto Imagawa.

They were primarily based in the Aichi state in

the Chubu region on the island of Honshu in

Japan.

They ruled until 1560 after the Battle of

Okehazama.

They were allies with the Takeda Clan and

Hojo Clan.

Saito Clan

The Saito Clan was a samurai clan during the Sengoku Period.

It was led by Yoshitatsu Saito.

They were primarily based in the Gifu state in the Chubu region on the island of Honshu in Japan.

They ruled until 1567 after they were defeated by Nobunaga Oda.

Date Clan

The Date Clan was a samurai clan during the

Sengoku Period.

It was led by Masamune Date.

They were primarily based in the Fukushima,

Miyagi, Iwate, and Aomori in the Tohoku

region on the island of Honshu in Japan.

They ruled until 1871 after the abolition of the

han system.

They were allies with the Tokugawa Clan.

Shimazu Clan

The Shimazu Clan was a samurai clan during the Sengoku Period.

It was led by Yoshihiro Shimazu.

They were primarily based in the Kagoshima and Miyazaki states on the island of Kyushu in Japan.

They ruled until 1947, after the Constitution of Japan rendered titles obsolete.

They were allies with the Tokugawa Clan.

Chosokabe Clan

The Chosokabe Clan was a samurai clan during

the Sengoku Period.

It was led by Motochika Chosokabe.

They were primarily based in the Kochi state on

the island of Shikoku in Japan.

They ruled until 1615 after the Siege on Osaka

Castle.

They were allies with the Miyoshi Clan and

Hosokawa Clan.

Azai Clan

The Azai Clan was a samurai clan during the Sengoku Period.

It was led by Nagamasa Azai.

They were primarily based in the Shiga state in the Kansai region on the island of Honshu in Japan.

They ruled until 1573 after Nagamasa Azai committed suicide.

Akechi Clan

The Akechi Clan was a samurai clan during the

Sengoku Period.

It was led by Mitsuhide Akechi.

They were primarily based in the Gifu state in

the Chubu region on the island of Honshu in

Japan.

They ruled until 1582 after the Battle of

Yamazaki.

They were former allies with the Oda Clan until

they betrayed Nobunaga Oda during the

Honnoji Incident

Sanada Clan

The Sanada Clan was a samurai clan during the Sengoku Period.

It was led by Masayuki Sanada.

They were primarily based in the Nagano state in the Chubu region on the island of Honshu in Japan.

They are still in existence even after their ruler Yukimura Sanada died in battle during the Siege of Osaka Castle in 1615.

Kuroda Clan

The Kuroda Clan was a samurai clan during the

Sengoku Period.

It was led by Kanbei Kuroda.

They were primarily based in the Shuzuoka

state in the Chubu region on the island of

Honshu in Japan.

They ruled until 1582 after the Battle of

Yamazaki.

They are still in existence to this day.

Tachibana Clan

The Tachibana Clan was a samurai clan during the Sengoku Period.

It was led by Ginchiyo Tachibana.

They were primarily based in the Fukouka state on the island of Kyushu in Japan.

They ruled until 1868 after the abolition of the han system.

They were allies with the Toyotomi Clan and Tokugawa Clan.

Warriors

Yoshimasa Ashikaga

Yoshimasa Ashikaga was the Shogun of Japan prior to the Sengoku Period.

Yoshimasa had an adopted son and son by birth.

When Yoshimasa retired as Shogun in 1473, a civil war broke out over which son would replace Yoshimasa as Shogun.

This conflict between two factions would lead to the Onin War that would start the Sengoku Period.

Yukimura Sanada

Yukimura Sanada was conisderd the greatest warrior of the land.

A master strategist and noble samurai, Yukimura was a fierce warrior for the Takeda and Toyotomi factions against the Oda and Tokugawa clans.

He would be defeated during the Battle of Osaka Castle in 1615, which would bring an end to the Sengoku Period.

Keiji Maeda

Keiji Maeda was a mercenary who allied with various clans and alliances.

He was a wild man wo acted like a kabuki and was unpredictable against a variety of opponents on the battlefield.

He was feared and respected for his strength and bravery.

The served in the Siege of Odawara and the Siege of Hasedo.

Nobunaga Oda

Nobunaga Oda was one of the Three Unifiers of Japan.

He believed in peace through violence and was on a warpath to take over Japan by any means necessary.

He would eventually be betrayed by one his retainers of the Akechi clan during the Honnoji Incident which led to his death.

His servant, Hideyoshi Toyotomi, would finish what he started.

Mitsuhide Akechi

Mitsuhide Akechi was one of Nobunaga Oda's most trusted vassals.

He served in various battles including the Battle of Nagaragawa, The Siege of Nagahsino, The Siege of Mount Hiei, The Battle of Tedorigawa, and the Battle of Yamazaki

However, he would betray Oda during the Honnoji incident which would lead to the fall of the Oda Clan as well as the death of Nobunaga Oda.

Goemon Ishikawa

Goemon Ishikawa was a legendary thief.

He would steal from the rich and give to the poor.

He was essentially a Japanese Robin Hood.

He was reportedly executed by boiling in 1594 after his failed assassination attempt on Hideyoshi Toyotomi.

He was also a legendary ninja and is considered an outlaw hero.

Kenshin Uesugi

Kenshin Uesugi was the leader of the Uesugi clan.

He was a devout Buddhist and a rival of the Shingen Takeda.

The participated in many battles during the Sengoku Period including the Battle of Saigawa, the Battle of Uenohara, the Siege of Odowara, The Battlae of Kwanakajima, the Siege of Karasawa, and the Battle of Tedorigawa.

He died in 1578.

Oichi Oda

Oichi Oda was Nobunaga's sister.

She was considered to be very intelligent and beautiful.

She also had multiple husbands including Nagamasa Azai and Katsuie Shibata.

She was also present during the Siege of Odani and the Siege of Kitanoshso which would lead to the extermination of the Azai Clan and Shibata Clan.

She was would later die in the Battle of Shizugatake in 1583.

Okuni Izumo

Okuni was an entertainer in Japan.

She is known for founding the Japanese dance style of Kabuki.

She was also a priestess and shrine maiden at the local Shinto temple in Izumo.

She was a popular performer and helped recruit an all female theater troupe over the Sengoku Period.

She died in 1613.

Magoichi Saika

Magoichi Saika was the leader of the Saika Renegades.

The was a ronin and may have had multiple identities.

He was like a real-life Dread Pirate Roberts.

He armed his troops with guns and donned the Yatagarasu, a three-legged crow, as his family crest.

He was a legendary pirate captain on par with Jack Sparrow.

He also participated in the Battle of Sekigahara.

Shingen Takeda

Shingen Takeda was an influential warlord in Japan.

He clashed with multiple war lords and was a master strategist.

He was the polar opposite and rival of Kenshin Uesugi.

He was known as the "Tiger" for his fierce battle style.

He later died in 1573 during the Siege of Noda Castle.

Masamune Date

Masamune Date was the head of the Date Clan.

He was known as the "one-eyed dragon" and an expert marksman.

He was also one of the wealthiest rulers of the Sengoku period.

He would serve the Tokugawa clan, and he originally opposed the outlawing of Christianity due to his support for foreigners.

He died in 1636 of cancer.

Lady No

Lady No was the wife of Nobunaga Oda.

Her marriage was a political truce between the

Oda and Saito clans.

Her death is subject to debate.

One points to her dying of illness.

One points to her being divorced from

Nobunaga and being banished as a result.

Another points to her dying in the Honnoji

Incident 1 in 1582.

Another points to her living up until 1612.

Hanzo Hattori

Hanzo Hattori was a legendary ninja, expert tactician, and master swordfighter.

He was an ally of the Tokugawa Clan during the Sengoku Period.

The fought in the Siege of Kakegawa, the Battle of Anegawa, the Battle of Komaki and Nagakute, and the Siege of Odawara.

He died in 1597, supposedly after being assassinated by rival ninja clan leader Kotaro Fuma.

Ranmaru Mori

Ranmaru Mori was the son of Yoshinari Mori.

He was considered very handsome and was a servant of Nobunaga Oda.

The was also considered one of Nobunaga Oda's bodyguards.

He died at a young age during the Honnoji Incident in 1582.

He was only 16 at the time of his death.

Hideyoshi Toyotomi

Hideyoshi Toyotomi was one of the Three Unifiers of Japan.

The started off as a peasant and servant of Nobunaga Oda before rising to power.

His agility, personality, and physique led him to be referred to as "Monkey".

After unifying Japan, he died suddenly due to illness.

His rags to riches story inspired other peasantry to rise up and achieve their dreams.

Yoshimoto Imagawa

Yoshimoto Imagawa was the leader of the Imagawa clan.

He had family relations with Shingen Takeda and Ujiyasu Hojo which the used to reign supreme as a master strategist and daimyo.

The fought in the battle of Azukizaka, the Battle of Muraki Castle, and the Battle of Okehazama.

He would eventually be killed in battle by Nobunaga Oda in 1560.

Tadakatsu Honda

Tadakatsu Honda was one of Ieyasu

Tokugawa's retainers.

He was a mighty and intelligent warrior who

was said to return from battle unharmed.

He was also the father of Lady Ina.

He was one of the Tokugawa Clan's Heavenly

Kings, along with Naomasa Ii, Yasumasa

Sakakibara and Tadatsugu Sakai.

He would participate Castle, the Siege of

Odawara and the Battle of Sekigahara.

Lady Ina

Lady Ina was Nobuyuki Sanada's wife and Yukimura Sanada's sister-in-law.

She was a master archer and served the Tokugawa Clan.

She took charge of sending food and other daily necessities to Masayuki Sanada and Yukimura Sanda when they were in exile after losing the Battle of Sekigahara.

She died of illness in 1620, a few years after the Siege of Osaka Castle.

Ieyasu Tokugawa

Ieyasu Tokugawa was one of the Three Unifiers of Japan.

He was a rival of the Toyotomi Clan after the fall of Nobunaga Oda and the Oda Clan.

The eventually defeated the Western Army in 1615, bringing an end to the Sengoku Period of Japan.

He was also prejudiced against Christians and would eventually ban Christianity in Japan.

He died of cancer shortly after unifying Japan in 1616.

Mitsunari Ishida

Mitsunari Ishida was one of the leaders of the Western Army.

He was a financial manager and helped manage the Toyotomi clan's war chest.

He participated in multiple battles, including the Siege of Takamatsy, the Battle of Shizugatake, and Japan's invasion of Korea.

He is known for leading the Western Army forces at the Battle of Sekigahara, where he died in battle in 1600.

Nagamasa Azai

Nagamasa Azai was Oichi Oda's husband.

He was involved in various battles including the

Siege on Kanegasaki, the Battle of Anegawa,

and the Siege of Odani Castle.

He would eventually help betray Nobunaga

Oda and was involved in plot that led to the

Honnoji Incident.

He died in 1573 before he could see the

Honnoji Incident for himself.

Sakon Shima

Sakon Shima was one of the leaders of the Western Army.

He served the Hatakeyama Clan, the Tsutsui Clan, and the Toyotomi Clan over many years during his military career.

He was a servant of Mitsunari Ishida and was also a wise and powerful general.

He died in 1600 during the Battle of Sekigahara.

Yoshihiro Shimazu

Yoshihiro Shimazu was the leader of the

Shimazu Clan.

He was a skilled general and helped contribute

to the unification of Kyushu and later Japan as a

whole.

He was known as "Devil" and helped

Hideyoshi invade Korea.

He later retired from warfare and taught the

next generation about warfare.

He died in 1619, a few years after the Siege of

Osaka Castle.

Ginchiyo Tachibana

Ginchiyo Tachibana was the leader of the Tachibana Clan.

She was an independent and strong woman who took over the clan after her father died.

She had as strong of a heart and will as any male clan leader during the Sengoku Period.

She participated in the unification of Kyushu and the Japanese invasion of Korea.

She died in 1602 a few years after the Siege of Yanagawa.

Kanetsugu Naoe

Kanetsugu Naoe was a retainer for the Uesugi Clan.

He helped convince Uesugi Clan leadership to join forces with the Toyotomi Clan to unify Japan.

He was also a faithful messenger and political spokesman.

He participated in the Battle of Tedorigawa, the Siege of Otate and the Odawara Campaign.

He died in 1620 a few years after the Siege of Osaka Castle.

Lady Nene

Lady Nene was Hideyoshi Toyotomi's wife.

She was also a nun and had cherished devotion to her husband.

She rose to political power after her husband died, and she also led all diplomatic affairs involving the imperial court.

She was also in charge of monitoring the daimyos families that were held hostage in Osaka Castle.

She died in 1624 a few years after the Siege of Osaka Castle.

Kataro Fuma

Kataro Fuma was a leader of a ninja clan.

He also served the Hojo Clan as one of its

retainers.

He participated in the Battle of Omosu and the

Siege of Odawara.

He and his ninjas were skilled at infiltration and

caused chaos in enemy camps.

He died in 1603 after being captured by the

Tokugawa Clan, where he was executed by

beheading.

Musashi Miyamoto

Musashi Miyamoto was one of Japan's greatest Swordsmen.

He dueled many warriors and wrote "The Book of Five Rings" as well as "The Path of Aloneness".

He also had many adopted children and a variety of students.

He died in 1645 years after the Shimabara rebellion.

Toshiie Maeda

Toshiie Maeda was one of Nobunaga Oda's generals.

He was a fierce warrior who would also serve the Toyotomi Clan.

He participated in the Battle of Ino, the Siege of Kanegasaki, The Battle of Anegawa, The Battle of Nagashino, the Battle of Tedorigawa, the Battle of Shizhugatake, and the Siege of Odawara among others.

He died in 1599 due to illness.

Motochika Chosokabe

Motochika Chosokabe was the leader of the

Chosokabe clan.

The conquered the entire Shikoku island with

his own resources.

He was known as "the Bat" because he refused

to travel away from his home.

He participated in the Battle of Nakatomigawa,

the Battle of Hiketa, the Kyushu Campaign, and

Japan's Invasion of Korea.

He died in 1599 a few years after the San Felipe

Incident.

Gracia Hosokawa

Gracia Hosokawa was Mitsuhide Akechi's daughter.

She was a devout Christian refused to be Mitsunari Ishida's hostage prior to the Battle of Sekigahara.

As a result, she accepted death by soldier rather than resort to suicide.

She died in 1600 after she was executed as a political hostage by Mitsunari Ishida.

Kojiro Sasaki

Kojiro Sasaki was a swordsman.

He was considered Musashi Miyamoto's greatest rival.

He is known for fending of three opponents with a tessen iron fan.

He was an expert in various forms of weapon, some being unconventional, including a laundry drying pole.

He later died in a duel in 1612.

Katsuie Shibata

Katsuie Shibata was one of Nobunaga Oda's generals.

He opposed Hideyoshi Toyotomi's rise to power after Nobunaga's death.

He was also one of Oichi Oda's husbands.

He served in the Battle of Ino, the Siege of Nagashima, the battle of Tedorigawa, and the Battle of Shuzugatake.

He died in 1583 shortly after the Honnoji Incident.

Kiyomasa Kato

Kiyomasa Kato was one of Hideyohsi

Toyotomi's generals.

He is known for being willing to assassinate

Ieyasu Tokugawa if he threatened to end

Hideyori Toyotomi on Kiyomasa's watch.

He was considered one of Hideyoshi

Toyotomi's Seven Spears of Shuzgatake along

with Masanori Fukushima, Nagayasu Hirano,

Takenori Kasuya, Katsumoto Katagiri,

Yoshiaki Kato and Yasuharu Wakizaka.

He died in 1611.

Kanbei Kuroda

Kanbei Kuroda was one of Hideyoshi

Toyotomi's strategists.

He is known for suffering years of

imprisonment when the failed peaceful

mediations with a rival clan.

While he did not have ambition, the Three

Unifiers feared that he could easily take Japan

for himself due to his intelligence.

He died in 1604 a few years after the Battle of

Sekigahara.

Muneshige Tachibana

Muneshige Tachibana was the husband of Ginchiyo Tachibana.

He was multi-talented and skillful.

He was also considered "a man amongst men".

Muneshige was also considered Tadakatsu Honda's equivalent.

He participated in the Kyusuhu Campaign, the Siege of Odawara, Japan's invasion of Korea, and the Siege of Osaka Castle.

He died in 1643 a few years after the Shimabara Rebellion.

Lady Kai

Lady Kai was a maiden of grace and beauty.

She was also very brave and cunning which was unusual for princesses at the time.

She would eventually become one of Hideysohi Toyotomi's concubines.

She volunteered to help defeat enemy soldiers attacking Oshi Castle and even engaged in battle with Mitsunari Ishida, Masayuki Sanada, and Nagamasa Asano.

This shamed the Toyotomi Clan for failing to capture a position guarded by a woman.

Ujiyasu Hojo

Ujiyasu Hojo was the leader of the Hojo Clan.

Referred to as "the Lion," he was revered as a

fearsome warrior and cunning man.

He was also very intelligent which helped him

create strategies to defeat both Kenshin Uesugi

and Shingen Takeda.

He was invoved in the Battle of Ozawahara, the

Siege of Matsuyama, and the Battle of

Numajiri.

He died in 1571, a few years after the Siege of

Odawara.

Hanbei Takenana

Hanbei Takenaka was a retainer who served

Hideyoshi.

He was a genius strategist and was referred to

as "All-knowing.".

He was also considered Kanbei Kuroda's rival.

He participated in the Battle of Nagaragawa,

the Siege of Inabayama the Battle of Anegawa,

and the Chugoku Campaign.

He died in 1579 shortly after the Siege of Miki.

Motonari Mori

Motonari Mori was the leader of the Mori Clan.

He was studious and wise and a master strategist.

He defended his clan from destruction through his large naval force.

He was involved in the Siege of Koriyama, the Battle of Oshikibata, the Battle of Miyajima, and the Siege of Tachibana.

He died in 1571 a few years after the Battle of Tatarahama.

Aya Uesugi

Aya Uesugi was Kenshin Uesugi's sister.

She was known for not wanting to participate in the Useugi Civil War that occurred over which heir should succeed Kenshin after his death.

She was also a devout Buddhist just like her brother.

She recommended Naoe Kanetsugu to serve the Uesugi as their advisor.

She died in 1609, a few years before the Siege of Osaka Castle.

Masanori Fukushima

Masanori Fukushima was a general who served Hideyoshi Toyotomi.

He was a powerful warrior and had a brazen temper.

Sometimes, he would go on murderous tantrums.

He participated in the Battle of Yamazaki, the Kyushu Campaign, Japan's Invasion of Korea, and the Battle of Sekigahara.

He died in 1624 a few years after surviving the Siege of Osaka Castle.

Takatora Todo

Takatora Todo was a daimyo who served

Ieyasu Tokugawa.

He was one of the Tokugawa Clan's most loyal

retainers.

He was also involved in the Tajima Campaign,

the Invasion of Shikoku, the Kyushu Campaign,

Japan's Invasion of Korea, the Battle of

Sekigahara, and the Siege of Osaka Castle.

He died in 1630 a few years before the

Shimabara Rebellion.

Naotora Ii

Naotora Ii was one the leader of the Ii Clan.

She was one of the last survivors of the

Imagawa Clan's mass killing of the Ii Clan.

Though a member of a minor clan, she was

known as "the Female landlord".

She was also Naomasa Ii's foster mother.

She was also an ally of the Tokugawa Clan and

had Naomasa Ii serve them as one of their

fiercest warriors.

She died in 1582 shortly after the Honnoji

Incident.

Muenori Yagyu

Muenori Yagyu was a famous swordsman.

He was also an instructor for the Tokugawa

Clan.

He was also a retainer for the Tokugawa Clan

and would later become one of their most

profitable vassals.

He was considered an unmatched duelist.

His sword style would eventually be patronized

by the Tokugawa Shogunate.

He died in 1646 a few years after the Shimabara

Rebellion.

Nobuyuki Sanada

Nobuyuki Sanada was Yukimura Sanada's brother and Lady Ina's husband.

He was also a servant of Hidetada Tokugawa.

His marriage was political, and he helped defeat the Western Army during the Battle of Sekigahara.

He was also involved in the Siege of Odawara and the Siege of Osaka Castle.

He died in 1658 at the age of 91 many years after the Shimabara Rebellion.

Yoshitsuga Otani

Yoshisuga Otani was Yukimura Sanda's father-in-law and one of Mitsunari Ishida's closest friends.

He would participate in tea ceremonies for the Toyotomi Clan and the Western Army.

This led to him meeting Mitsunari Ishida, and they became very close friends.

He also suffered from leprosy.

Despite this, he was a loyal friend who kept his promises until he was killed during the Battle of Sekigahara in 1600.

Lady Chikurinin

Lady Chikurinin was Yukimura Sanada's wife and the daughter in law of Yoshisuga Otani.

She was also the adopted daughter of Hideyoshi Toyotomi.

She also took care of her husband while the was exiled to Mt. Koya after losing the Battle of Sekigahara.

She was once captured by Nagaakira Asano and handed over to the Tokugawa, but was spared.

She died in 1649 yeas after the Shimabara Rebellion.

Hisahide Matsunaga

Hisahide Matsunaga was a retainer for the Oda

Clan.

He was once a retainer for the Nagayoshi

Miyoshi and even conspired against his master

for personal gain.

He was infamous for being cruel, violent, and

cunning.

He is accredited for killing the shogun,

Yoshiteru Ashikaga.

He died in 1577 during the Siege of Shigisan.

Kojuro Katakura

Kojuro Katakura was as strategist who served Masamune Date.

He had a valuable wit and was known as "the Wise".

He was also a talented musician who played the flute.

He was involved in the Siege of Odawara, the Battle of Hasedo, and the Kasai-Osaki Uprising.

He died in 1615, shortly after the Siege of Osaka Castle.

Kagekatsu Uesugi

Kagekatu Uesugi was one of Kenshin's adopted sons.

He is also Lady Aya's biological son.

The allied with Mitsunari Ishida during the battle of Sekigahara.

He was involved in the Battle of Tedorigawa, the Siege of Otate, the Siege of Uozu, the Siege of Hachioji, and the Battle of Sekigahrara.

He died in 1623 a few years after the Siege of Osaka Castle.

Takakage Kobayakawa

Takakage Kobayakawa was Motonari Mori's son.

He and his brother, Motoharu Kikkawa, were responsible for raising Motonari Mori's grandson, Terumoto Mori.

Takakage was viewed as strict and harsh.

He was involed in the Invasion of Shikoku, the Siege of Odawra, and the Kyushu Campaign.

He died in 1597, shortly after Japan's Invasion of Korea.

Lady Koshosho

Lady Koshosho was Mitochika Chosokabe's
concubine.

She was considered an evil wench that was
viewed as adulterous and condescending.

She married various people for convenience
and would be seen walking with different men
in a heartbeat.

She was also Mochitaka Hosokawa's concubine
at one point in time.

She also served as Yoshikata Miyoshi's
concubine as well.

Toyohisa Shimazu

Toyohisa Shimazu was Yoshihiro Shimazu's nephew.

He was once considered a future candidate to lead the Shimazu Clan.

He was considered a bold and steadfast general.

He participated in he Battle of Okitanawate, the Kyushu Campaign, the Siege of Odawara, and Japan's Invasion of Korea.

He died in 1600 during the Battle of Sekigahara.

Lady Hayakawa

Lady Hayawaka was Uhiyasu Hojo's daughter.

She was also Ujizane Imagawa's wife.

She married into the Imagwa clan as a
condition of the Kososhun Triple Alliance
between the Takeda Clan, Hojo Clan and
Imagawa Clan.

After the Takeda broke the alliance, she ran
away with Ujizane Imagawa to join the
Tokugawa Clan.

She died in 1613 shortly before the Siege of
Osaka Castle.

Naomasa Ii

Naomasa Ii was a loyal vassal of Ieyasu Tokugawa.

He wore bright red armor to make it known he was on the battlefield.

He was known as the "Red Devil" and was both feared and respected.

He participated in the Siege of Takatenjin, the Siege of Odawara, and the Battle of Gifu Castle.

He died in 1602 shortly after the Battle of Sekigahara.

Masayuki Sanada

Masayuki Sanada was Lady Muramatsu,

Nobuyuki Sanada and Yukimura Sanada's

father.

He was a shred and master strategist.

He was known for stopping Hidetada

Tokugawa's army of 38,000 with just 2,000

soldiers at the battle of Ueda Castle.

He was known for being cunning and sly as

well as a quick thinker.

He died of illness in 1611 during his exile to

Mt. Kudoyama.

Lady Muramatsu

Lady Muramatsu was Nobyuki Sanada and

Yukimura Sanada's sister.

She was highly respected, and she would

exchange letters with her brothers while they

were on military campaigns.

She was also, at one point, a political hostage of

Nobunaga Oda's until she was freed during the

Honnoji Incident.

She died in 1630 a few years before the

Shimabara Rebellion.

Lady Chacha

Lady Chacha was Hideyoshi Toyotomi's concubine and Hideyori Toyotomi's mother.

She was the de facto head of Osaka castle after Hideyoshi's death.

She had incredible political influence and was considered potential enemy for the Tokugawa Clan.

She died in 1615 during the Siege of Osaka Castle.

Katsuyori Takeda

Katsuyori Takeda was Shingen Takeda's son.

The hadearly accomplishments in his military career.

However, he was responsible for losing the Battle of Nagashino which brought ruin to the Takeda Clan.

He participated in the Siege of Kanbara, the Siege of Futamata, the Siege of Yoshida, and the Battle of Omasu.

He died in 1582 during the Battle of Tenmokuzan.

Hidetada Tokugawa

Hidetada Tokugawa was Ieyasu Tokugawa's son and successor.

He lost horribly to the Sanada army at Ueda castle.

As a result of his own vendetta against the Sanada Clan, he was unable to assist the Eastern Army during the Battle of Sekigahara, costing him his relationship with his father.

He died in 1632 a few years before the Shimabara Rebellion.

Toshimitsu Saito

Toshimitsu Saito was one of Mitsuhide

Akechi's most trusted retainers.

He was a loyal warrior and his skills were

recognized by Nobunaga Oda.

He was the father of Lady Kasuga.

He was involved in the Tanba Campaign, the

Siege of Kuroi Castle, the Honnoji Incident,

and the Battle of Yamazaki.

He died in 1582.

Lady Sena

Lady Sena was the adopted daughter of Yoshimoto Imagawa.

She would eventually become Ieyasu Tokugawa's wife.

She was known for initiating a conspiracy against Nobunaga Oda for her husband's benefit.

This led to the Anti-Oda coalition.

She died in 1579 after being beheaded for treason by the Tokugawa Clan.

Kazuuji Nakamura

Kazuuji Nakamura was a general of Hideyoshi Toyotomi.

He was also an arbiter that settled disputes.

He fought in the Battle of Komaki-Nagakute and the Kishu Campaign.

After Hideyoshi's death, he would go on to serve the Tokugawa Clan.

He died of illness in 1600, shortly before the Battle of Sekigahara started.

Shikanosuke Yamanaka

Shikanosuke Yamanaka was a general in the Amago Clan.

He was very courageous and known as "the Kirin" (or Asian Chimera).

He is known for resisting the Mori Clan and trying to restore the Amago Clan until his death.

He participated in the Siege of Gassantoda Castle and the Battle of Fubeyama.

He died in 1578, during the Siege of Kozuki Castle.

Yasuke

Yasuke was a vassal who served Nobunaga Oda.

A former African slave under the Jesuit Allessandro Valignano, he would eventually escape to freedom and become a legendary samurai.

His exotic appearance caused much controversy and became a legend in Japan.

He was involved in the Battle of Tenmokuzan and the Honnoji Incident.

Sandayu Momochi

Sandayu Momochi was a ninja leader.

He defied Nobungaa Oda during the riots in

Iga.

He is also considered the teacher and mentor of

Goemon Ishikawa.

In 1581, Iga was invaded by the Oda Clan, and

no man, woman, or child was spared.

It is unknown if Sandayu Momochi survived

the slaughter or not.

Nobuyuki Oda

Nobuyuki Oda was Nobunaga Oda's brother.

He participated in the Battle of Ino.

He was involved in a brief civil conflict with his brother over the leadership of the Oda Clan in 1558.

As a result of his conspiracy against Nobunaga, Nobuyuki was executed for treason by his own brother.

He was 21 at the time of his death.

Dosan Saito

Dosan Saito was Lady No and Yoshitatsu

Saito's father.

He was known as "the Viper" and had his

daughter marry Nobunaga Oda in order to

forma truce between the Oda and Saito Clans.

He participated in the Mino Campaign and the

Battle of Kanoguchi.

He died in 1556, during the Battle of

Nagaragawa.

Yoshitatsu Saito

Yoshitatsu Saito was the Dosan Saito's successor and Tatsuoki Saito's father.

He is known for defeating his father at the Battle of Nagaragawa and wiping out any opposition within the clan so he could declare himself the second head of the Saito clan.

He participated in the Battle of Nagaragawa in 1556.

He died in 1561.

Yoshikage Asakura

Yoshikage Asakura was the leader of the

Asakura Clan.

He was an expert negotiator and was a skilled

political and diplomatic manager.

He participated in the Siege of Kanegasaki the

Battle of Anegawa, and the Siege of Hikida

Castle.

He led a major Anti-Oda coalition until his

death at the Battle of Ichijodani Castle in 1573.

Motonobu Okabe

Motonobu Okabe was a retainer for the Imagawa Clan.

He was known for retrieving Yoshimoto Imagawa's body after the was killed by Nobunaga Oda.

He participated in the Battle of Okehazama.

He would swiutch allegiance to the Takeda Clan after the Imagawa Clan's collapse.

He would later be killed in battle by Tadakatsu Honda's siege of Takatenjin Castle.

Yoshiaki Ashikaga

Yoshiaki Ashikaga was a former member of the Ashikaga Shogunate.

He is famous for dealing with several daimyo during the Sengoku Period.

The also organized a coalition of generals to try and kill Nobunaga Oda.

However, he lost his seat in power after Nobunaga drove him out of the capital during Nobunaga's March to Kyoto.

He died in 1597.

Fujihide Mitsubishi

Fujihide Mitsubuchi was a guardian of Yoshiaki Ashikaga.

The was a liason between Nobunaga's forces and the Ashikaga Shogunate.

He tried to reclaim the shogun's power from Nobunaga Oda.

However, his plot was discovered and he was ordered to commit suicide under the supervision of Mitsuhide Akechi.

He died in 1574.

Terumoto Mori

Terumoto Mori was Motonari Mori's grandson.

He was a general of Hideyoshi Toyotomi and was part of the five elders along with Hideie Uktia, Toshiie Maeda, Kagekatsu Uesugi, and ieayasiu Tokugawa.

He participated in the Battle of Fubeyama, the Ishiyama Honganji War, Japan's Invasion of Korea, and the Battle of Sekigahara.

He died in 1625 years after the Siege of Osaka Castle.

Hideie Ukita

Hideie Ukita was one of five elders appointed by Hideyoshi Toyotomi to take care of his heir, after Hideyoshi's death.

He participated in the Kyushu Campaign, the Siege of Odawara, and Japan's Invasion of Korea.

He saved Mitsunari Ishida from assassination and joined the Western Army at the Battle of Sekigahara.

He died in 1655.

Motoharu Kikkawa

Motoharu Kikkawa was Motonari Mori's son.

He and his brother, Takakage Kobayakwa, were responsible for raising Motonari Mori's grandson, Terumoto Mori.

Motoharu was viewed as strong and fearless.

He participated in the Battle of Miyajima, the Siege of Toda Castle, the Battle of Tatarahama, the Siege of Kozuki Castle, and the invasion of Shikoku.

He died in 1586.

Hideyori Toyotomi

Hideyori Toyotomi was the son of Hideysohi Toyotomi.

He was the leader of the Western Army and was one of the successors for Shogun along with Ieyasu Tokugawa of the Eastern Army.

He committed suicide after setting Osaka Castle on fire because he did not want to admit defeat to the Eastern Army during the Siege of Osaka Castle.

William Adams

William Adams was an English navigator who

was the first Englishman to reach Japan in

1600.

He was also the first Englishman to travel to

Thailand and Vietnam.

He would become an advisor to Ieaysu

Tokugawa and was one of the first Western

Samurai.

He died in 1620, a few years after the Siege of

Osaka Castle.

Joao Rodrigues

Joao Rodrigues was a Portuguese sailor and a Jesuit priest.

He acted as an international translator between the Japanese, English, and Chinese.

He wrote the book "The Art of the Japanese Language".

He also helped introduce western science and culture to Korea.

He died in 1633 while on a mission in China.

Yukinaga Konishi

Yukinaga Konishi was a daimyo who served

Hideyoshi Toyotomi.

He was a devout Christian and acted as

vanguard during the Japanese invasion of

Korea.

He participated in the Siege of Takamatsu, the

Siege of Ota Castle, the Invasion of Shikoku,

the Kyushu Campaign, Japan's Invasion of

Korea, and the Battle of Sekigahara.

He died in 1600.

Tadaoki Hosokawa

Hosokawa Tadaoki was Gracia Hosokawa's husband.

He was a vanguard for the Tokugawa clan during the Battle of Sekigahara and was also involved in the Siege of Osaka castle.

He was involved in the Odawara Campaign, Japan's Invasion of Korea, the Battle of Sekigahara, and the Siege of Osaka Castle.

He died in 1646 a few years after the Shimabara Rebellion.

Allessandro Valignano

Allessandro Valignanao was Yasuke's slave

master and an Italian Jesuit priest.

He helped introduce Catholicism and

Christianity to the Far East, especially in Japan.

He also helped introduce Catholicism to India,

and China as well.

He was also involved in the establishment of

the Port of Nagaski, bringing missionaries and

foreign trade to Japan.

He died in 1606 a few years after the Battle of

Sekigahara.

Lady Acha

Lady Acha was a concubine of Ieyasu

Tokugawa.

She was very intelligent and managed the

Tokugawa Clan's family affairs.

She was also sent to negotiate peace during the

Siege of Osaka Castle.

She was also a devout Buddhist.

She died in 1637 a year before the Shimabara

Rebellion.

Masamoto Hosokawa

Masamoto Hosokawa was the deputy shogun of Japan.

He was known for overthrowing the Ashikaga Shogunate from power in the Meio Incident.

He would then choose someone else to be his successor, and as a result, he was assassinated by two of his retainers.

He died in 1507 after being killed by Motonaga Kosai and Sumiyuki Hosakawa while he was taking a bath.

Harukata Sue

Harukata Sue was a samurai and retainer for the Ouchi Clan.

He is known for leading a coup against Yoshitaka Ouchi leading to the Taeneiji Incident.

He was also involved in the Battle of Miyajima, the Battle of Oshikibata, and the Battle of Itsukushima.

He died in 1555 after committing suicide.

Yoshitaka Ouchi

Yoshitaka Ouchi was the leader of the Ouchi

Clan.

He is known for being betrayed by Harukata

Sue during the Taeneiji Incident.

He was also involved in the Siege of Toda

Castle and the Taineiji Incident.

After his ministers and courtiers were

massacred by Sue Clan, he died in 1551 after

committing suicide and composing a death

poem.

Nagayoshi Miyoshi

Nagayoshi Miyoshi was a powerful daimyo.

He engaged in military campaigns and rose to power against the Rokakku Clan and Hosakawa Clan.

He was involved in many battles and wars including the Battle of Kyokoji.

He even defeated the then shogun Yoshiteru Ashikaga and banished him in 1558.

He died in 1564.

Events

The Sengoku Period was a Japanese Civil War across different states and clans for over 150 years.

The start of it can be traced back to 1454 to during the Kyotoku Incident, Onin War in 1467, and the Meio Incident in 1493.

The end of it can be traced back to 1600 during the Battle of Sekigahara, the Siege of Osaka Castle in 1615, and even the Shimabara Rebellion in 1638.

Kyotoku Incident

The Kyotoku Incident occurred in 1454 and

lasted until 1482.

It involved a series of skirmishes and conflicts

for control of the Kanto region and ended when

the Ashikaga, Uesugi, and Imagawa clans

negotiated peace with each other for a brief

period of time.

It was essentially the prologue to the Sengoku

period.

Onin War

The Onin War occurred in 1467 and lasted until 1477.

It was a civil war that led to Kyoto, Japan's capital at the time, being destroyed and disintegration of the power of the Shogunate.

The Hosakawa Clan won the war and it led to the Ouchi Clan abandoning Kyoto.

Yoshihisa Ashikaga would become shogun as a result.

It was the beginning of the Sengoku Period in Japan.

Yamashiro Uprising

The Yamashiro Uprising occurred in 1485.

It led to the creation of a confederacy by

multiple samurai armies.

It would lead to the creation of the Yamashiro

Ikki as well as a military and civil

confederation of various clans.

It was also used to eventually combat the

spread of Christianity and be a safe haven for

Buddhists and followers of Shintoism.

Battle of Magari

The Battle of Magari occurred in 1487.

It led to the Shogun, Yoshihisa Ashikaga to be wounded and defeated by the Rokkaku Clan.

It was also a joint operation between the Iga and Koka ninja clans in a mutual defense of their homeland.

These ninja clans participated in hit-and-run tactics and night attacks, among other forms of guerilla warfare, to oppose the rule of the Shogunate.

Kaga Rebellion

The Kaga Rebellion occurred in 1488.

It led to the Ikko-ikki gaining control of Kaga

and defeating the Togashi Clan.

The Ikko-ikki forces were 200,000 and were

able to kill the opposing commanding officer,

Masachika Togashi.

It would also lead to Yasutaka Togashi to

become military governor of the stte of

Ishikawa in the Chubu Region on the Island of

Honshu in Japan.

Puppetization of the Ashikaga Shogunate

The Puppetiztion of the Ashikaga Shogunate occurred in 1492.

This happened when Yoshiaki Ashikaga was installed as Shogun so he could be Nobunaga Oda's convenient puppet for political and military reasons.

This would eventually lead to the Hosokawa Clan, the Miyoshi Clan, and Ashikaga Clan forming an alliance to try and stop Nobunaga Oda's rise to power.

Meio Incident

The Meio Incident occurred in 1493.

It involved the Ashikaga being dethroned in a coup led by Masamoto Hosokawa.

This led to Masamoto Hosakawa taking over the Shogunate.

This would elad to corruption of power and eventually lead to the Taineiji Incident as a result of anti-Hosakawa sentiment among the population.

The Ryo Kosokawa War

The Ryo Koskawa War occurred in 1507.

It involved a succession dispute in the

Hosokawa Family.

It eventually led to the assassination of

Masamoto Hosokawa in his bathtub by two of

his retainers.

This would eventually lead to Sumiyuki

Hosakawa forcing the Shogunate to recognize

him as the head of the Hosokawa Clan and as

Shogun of Japan.

Battle of Arita-Nakaide

The Battle of Arita-Nakaide occurred in 1517.

It occurred in the Hiroshima State in the

Chugoku Region on the Island of Honshu in

Japan.

It involved the Mori Clan defeating the Takeda

Clan.

The Mori Clan also had assistance from the

Yoshikawa Clan as well.

It was also Motonari Mori's first battle.

Suspension of Chinese Relations with Japan

The Suspension of Chinese Relations with Japan occurred in 1523.

This was due to the civil war that was occurring in Japan for over 60 years.

It was not until after the Ming Dynasty collapsed and after the Sengoku Period in 1662 that diplomatic relations would restart between the two countries.

Battle of Idano

The Battle of Idano occurred in 1535.

It was fought in the Aichi State in the Chubu

Region on the Island of Honshu in Japan

This led to the Matsudaira forces defeating the

rebel Masatoyo forces.

Siege of Koriyama

The Siege of Koriyama occurred in 1541.

It resulted in the Amago clan being defeated by the Ouchi and Mori clans.

The Amago clan had 30,000 troops while the Mori Clan and Ouchi Clan only had 18,000 troops combined.

Portuguese Land in Japan

The Portuguese landed in Japan in 1543.

They brought matchlock guns, which

dramatically changed the warfare between clans

in Japan.

The Portuguese ese were the first Europeans to

arrive in Japan.

They also brought Christianity to the island

nation of Japan as well.

The Siege of Kawagoe Castle

The Siege of Kawagoe Castle occurred from 1545 to 1546.

It took place in the Saitama State in the Kanto Region, on the Island of Honshu in Japan.

This led to Ujiyasu Hogo to defeat the Uesugi Clana and become the ruler of the Kanto region.

Taineiji Incident

The Taineiji Incident occurred in 1551.

This involved Harukata Sue betraying

Yoshitaka Ouchi, which led to Harukata taking

control of western Honshu.

It took place in the Yamaguchi State in the

Chugoku Region on the Island of Honshu in

Japan.

The Kososhun Triple Alliance

The Kososhun Triple Alliance was established in 1554.

It was formed between the Takeda, Hojo, and Imagawa Clans.

It was also established to form peace between the three clans and allow reinforcements and support for each other if one of them was attacked.

Battle of Kawanakajima

The Battle of Kawanakajima occurred from

1553 to 1564.

It was as series of battles between the Takeda

and Uesugi clans.

It resulted in constant stalemates.

The fourth battle was a tactical victory for the

Uesugi Clan, but it was also a strategic victory

for the Takeda Clan.

Invasion of Suruga

The invasion of Suruga occurred from 1554 and 1568.

It resulted in the Takeda Clan defeating the Hojo Clan, Uesugi Clan and the Imagawa Clan.

The Takeda Clan broke the peace treaty between them and the Hojo clan.

This was done through influence and assistance by the Tokugawa Clan

Battle of Itsukushima

The Battle of Itsukushima occurred in 1555.

It resulted in the Mori Clan defeating the Sue Clan.

The Mori Clan was able to defeat the Sue Clan, despite the Sue Clan having more than four times as many troops as the Mori Clan.

This led to the Mori conquering Japan's Holy Land for Shintoism.

Battle of Nagaragawa

The Battle of Nagaragawa occurred in 1556.

It took place in the Gifu State in the Chubu

Region on the Island of Honshu in Japan.

It was a brief civil war fought among the Saito

Clan.

It resulted in the Dosan Saito being killed by

Yoshitatsu Saito.

Battle of Okehazama

The Battle of Okehazama occurred in 1560.

It took place in the Aichi State in the Chubu

Region on the Island of Honshu in Japan.

It resulted in the Oda Clan defeating the

Imagawa Clan.

It also led to Yoshimoto Imagawa being killed

in battle destroying the Imagawa Clan.

The Great Kanto Defense

The Great Kanto Defense occurred from 1560

to 1561.

It resulted in the Hojo Clan defeating the

Useugi Clan.

It would eventually lead to more conflict among

the different clans in the Kanto Region of Japan

among the Takeda Clan, Usugi Clan, and Hojo

Clan after the collapse of the Imagawa Clan by

Nobunaga Oda.

The Battle of Odawara Castle

The Battle of Odawara Castle occurred in 1561.

It resulted in The Uesugi Clan withdrawing

from battle against the Hojo Clan.

The castle town of Odawara would eventually

be burned to the ground by the Uesugi.

The Uesugi Clan had over 110,000 troops while

the Hojo clan was able to defend their town

with only 15,000 troops.

Siege of Moji

The Siege of Moji occurred in 1561.

It involved the Mori Clan defeating the Otomo

Clan.

This battle is significant as the Otomo Clan was

also aided by the Portuguese showing one of

the first signs of western meddling among the

different clans during the Sengoku Period.

Defense of Echizen

The Defense of Echizen occurred in 1563.

It involved in the Awaya Clan defeating the Asakura Clan.

This was primarily done to stop a rebellion that was taking place as far back as 1561.

This would eventually lead to Yoshikage Asakura losing control of Echizen and admitting defeat to Katsuhisa Awaya.

Battle of Fukuda Bay

The Battle of Fukuda Bay occurred in 1565.

It involved the Portuguese Empire defeating the Matsura Clan.

It was the first major Portuguese victory against Japanese forces during the Sengoku Period.

It led to the destruction of the Matsura Clan's Navy and also led to the Portuguese expanding their influence to the state of Nagasaki and the island of Kyushu.

Siege of Inabayama Castle

The Siege of Inabayama Castle occurred in 1567.

It resulted in the Oda Clan defeating the Saito Clan.

This would also lead to Inabayama Castle falling to Nobunaga Oda, providing a great castle garrison with a mountain top vantage point for the Oda Clan.

Siege of Gassantoda Castle

The Siege of Gassantoda Castle occurred from 1542 until 1569.

It took place over three different sieges of the castle

It resulted the Mori Clan defeating the Amago Clan.

It also led to the Mori Clan gaining control of Gassantoda Castle near the Japanese Coast.

Battle of Kannonji Castle

The Battle of Kannonji Castle occurred in 1568.

It resulted in the Oda Clan defeating the

Rokkaku Clan.

Kannonji Castle is considered one of Japan's

Five Great Mountain Castles along with

Kasugayama Castle, Nanao Castle, Odani

Castle, and Gassantoda Castle.

Nobunaga Oda's March toward Kyoto

Nobunaga Oda's March toward Kyoto occurred in 1568.

It led to the Nobunaga Oda overthrowing Yoshihide Ashikaga.

It was similar to Sherman's March to the Sea during the American Civil War, with countless deaths and destruction in Nobunaga Oda's war path.

Battle of Rokuji

The Battle of Rokuji occurred in 1569.

It resulted in the Oda Clan defeating the

Miyoshi Clan.

This would lead to the Honkokuji Temple

Incident, where the Imperial Palace was burned

down and the Miyoshi Triumvirate killed

Yoshiteru Ashikaga, the Shogun at the time.

Battle of Mimase Pass

The Battle of Mimase Pass occurred in 1569.

It resulted in the Takeda Clan defeating the

Hojo Clan.

This was significant as the Takeda Clan only

had 10,000 troops while the Hojo Clan had

20,000 troops.

This showed the Takeda Clan's resourcefulness

and efficiency with a limited number of troops.

Retreat from Kanegasaki

The Retreat from Kanegasaki occurred in 1570.

It resulted in the Oda Clan and Tokugawa Clan successfully retreating from the Azai Clan and Asakura Clan.

This was significant as the Oda Clan and Tokugawa Clan had a combined force of 30,000, yet they were defeated by the Azai Clan and Asakura Clan, who only had 24,000 troops.

Battle of Anegawa

The Battle of Anegawa occurred in 1570.

It resulted in the Oda Clan and Tokugawa Clan defeating the Azai Clan and Asakura Clan.

This was significant as the Oda Clan and Tokugawa Clan had a combined total of 28,000 troops, and they were able to defeat the Azai and Asakura Clans, who only had 18,000 troops.

This was considered a payback war for the previous Retreat from Kanegasaki.

Ishiyama Honganji War

The Ishiyama Honganji War occurred from

1570 to 1580.

It resulted in the Oda Clan defeating the

Ashikaga Clan, Yoshiaki Clan, and Mori Clan.

This also led to Honganji Clan surrendering to

the Oda Clan.

The Oda Clan forces totaled 30,000 while the

Ashikaga Clan, Yoshiaki Clan and Mori Clan

forces only totaled 15,000.

Portuguese Establish Trade in Nagasaki

The Portuguese established Trade in Nagasaki in 1571.

This was significant as it established a physical base of operation for Portuguese influence as well as the spread of the Catholic Church in Japan.

While Nagasaki was on the island of Kyushu off the mainland of Japan, the influence of the Portuguese and Catholic Church would eventually spread to the Island of Honshu.

Siege of Mount Hiei

The Siege of Munt Hiei occurred in 1571.

It resulted in the Oda clan defeating the Sohei

monks.

This was significant as it showed Nobunaga

Oda's opposition to religion, particularly

Buddhism, which opposed his violent rule.

There were no survivors of Buddhist monks

during Nobunaga Oda's slaughter of the Sohei

monks.

End of the Ashikaga Shogunate

The End of the Ashikaga Shogunate occurred in 1573.

This happened as a result of Yoshiaki Ashikaga who staged a revolt and was overthrown by Nobunaga Oda.

The Oda Clan's 30,000 troops defeated the Ashikaga Clan, the Matsunaga Clan and the Takeda Clan.

Battle of Mikatagahara

The Battle of Mikatagahara occurred in 1573.

It resulted in the Tokugawa Clan retreating

from the Takeda Clan.

The Oda Clan was also involved on the side of

the Tokugawa Clan.

The Takeda Clan's 35,000 troops easily

defeated the Tokugawa and Oda Clan's 11,000

troops who were almost annihilated.

Siege of Odani Castle

The siege of Odani Castle occurred in 1573.

It resulted in the Oda Clan defeating the Azai

Clan.

The Oda Clan forces had 30,000 troops while

the Azai Clan only had 5000 troops.

It was a major comeback victory for Nobunaga

Oda.

Abolition of the Muromachi Shogunate

The Abolition of the Muromachi Shogunate occurred in 1573.

This occurred when Yoshiaki Ashikaga was driven out of Kyoto by Nobunaga Oda.

This would end Muromachi Shogunate and lead to a country without a Shogun.

This era of a leaderless state lasted 9 years until the Akechi Clan took over the Shogunate after they killed Nobunaga Oda during the Honnoji Incident.

Rokkaku and Koka surrender to Nobunaga Oda

Rokkaku and Koka surrendered to Nobunaga Oda in 1574.

This was significant as it meant Nobunaga Oda now had a ninja army at his command, making the assassination of the opposition even easier for him to achieve.

Siege of Nagashima

The Siege of Nagashima occurred from 1571 to 1574.

It took place over three sieges.

It resulted in the Oda Clan killing the entire Ikko Ikki population of Buddhist Monks and the complete destruction of the Nagashima Complex.

This event showed Nobunaga Oda's willingness to commit genocide against Buddhists and led to a public outcry against Nobunga's rule.

Battle of Nagashino

The Battle of Nagahsino occurred in 1575.

It resulted in the Takeda Clan being crippled by the Oda Clan and Tokugawa Clan.

This led to Nobunaga Oda being very close to achieving unification in Japan.

Siege of Nanao

The Siege of Nanao occurred in 1577.

It resulted in the Uesugi Clan defeating the

Hatakeyama Clan.

It was significant as Nanao Castle fell to the

Uesugi Clan, giving them a tactical advantage

by having a mountain near the castle as one of

their bases.

The Battle of Tedorigawa

The Battle of Tedorigawa occurred in 1577.

It resulted in the Uesugi Clan defeating the Oda Clan.

This was significant as the Uesugi Clan only had 30,000 troops while the Oda Clan had 50,000 troops.

Most of the Oda's men were lost by drowing after crossing the Tedori River in the freezing cold.

It was similar to Napoleon's failed invasion of Russia.

Battle of Kizugawaguchi

The Battle of Kizigawaguchi occurred from 1576 to 1578.

It led to the Oda Clan defeating the Mori Clan.

It was significant as the first battle showed the power of the Oda Clan's small Navy 7 ships and they were able to defeat the Mori Clan's 600 ships with limited resources.

Battle of Kasugayama Castle

The Battle of Ksagayama Castle occurred from 1578 to 1579.

It resulted in Kagetora Uesugi retreating and Kagekatsu Uesugi claiming the castle.

This would lead to Kagekatsu Uesugi taking over the Uesugi Clan and becoming the new head of the family.

Siege of Kozuki Castle

The Siege of Kozuki Castle occurred in 1578.

It resulted in the Mori Clan defeating the Oda

Clan.

Its heavily believed that Yukimori Yamanaka

sold Katsuhisa Amago's life to save his own

when he surrendered.

Sena's Letter to Takeda.

Sena sent a letter to the Takeda Clan to form an alliance against the Oda Clan in 1579.

This was a result of Nobunaga Oda killer her father, Yoshimoto Imagawa and Lady Sena wanting revenge against the Oda Clan.

It was similar to the Zimmeran Note between Germany and Mexico against the United States that would lead the United States getting involved in World War I.

Subjugation of Shikoku

The Subjugation of Shikoku occurred from 1581 to 1585.

There was original a break in the military campaign in 1582 due to the Honnoji Incident taking place.

It resulted in the Chosokabe Clan surrendering to the Hashiba Clan in 1585.

This would lead to Hideyoshi Toyotomi marching west to the island of Shikoku and taking it over.

Tensho Iga Wars

The Tensho Iga Wars occurred from 1579 to 1581.

The first war occurred in 1579 that led to the Iga defeating the Oda Clan and maintaining its independence from the Shogunate.

The second war occurred in 1581 and resulted in the Oda Clan conquering Iga and pacifying all rebel forces in the area.

This would lead to Nobunaga Oda having control of the Iga ninja army and be able to use them for espionage and guerilla tactics.

The Honnoji Incident

The Honnoji Incident occurred on June 21, 1582.

It resulted in Mitsuhide Akechi betraying Nobunaga Oda, which resulted in Nobunaga's assassination and the fall of the Oda Clan.

Many other high ranking officials in the Oda clan were also killed.

This would lead to the creation of the Akechi Shogunate;

It was similar to the ides of March in Ancient Rome.

Battle of Yamazaki

The Battle of Yamazaki occurred in 1582.

It resulted in the Hashiba Clan defeating the

Akechi Clan and Mitsuhide Akechi's death.

It would also jump start Hideyoshi Toyotomi's

consolidation of power from the remnants of

the Oda Clan and eventually taking over

Nobunaga Oda's authority and power toward

unification of Japan.

Battle of Mount Tenmoku

The Battle of Mount Tenmoku occurred in 1582.

It resulted in the Oda Clan putting an end to the Takeda Clan.

It was the Tekada Clan's last stand for survival and resulted in the death of their leader, Katsuyori Takeda.

The entire 40-man army of the Takeda Clan was destroyed by the Oda Clan and Tokugawa Clan's 4000 troops.

Battle of Shizugatake

The Battle of Shizugatake occurred in 1583.

It resulted in the Toyotomi Clan defeating the

Shibata clan and Katsuie Shibata's death.

The Toyotomi Clan's forces totaled 50,000

troops, while the combined forces of the

Shibata Clan only had 30,000 troops.

This was a decisive victory for Hideyoshi

Toyotomi that started a domino effect of clan

surrenders that would eventually lead to the

unification of Japan.

Occupation of Shikoku

Motochika Chosokabe extended his power to all of the island of Shikoku in 1583

This was significant as the entire island of Shikoku was under the rule of the Chosokabe Clan.

It would not be until 1585 that Shikoku would be conquered by the Hideyoshi Toyotomi and the Toyotomi Clan as part of their campaign for unification of all of the islands of Japan.

Battle of Komaki and Nagakute

The Battle of Komaki and Nagakute occurred in 1584.

It resulted in peace negotiations between the Toyotomi Clan and the Tokugawa Clan. Both Ieyasu Tokugawa and Hideyoshi Toyotomi served Nobunaga Oda, so the peace negotiations were for the common goal of unifying Japan, as Nobunaga Oda originally wanted to do.

Occupation of Kyushu

Yoshihisa Shimazu extended his power to all of

the island of Kyushu in 1584

This was significant as the entire island of

Kyushu was under the rule of the Shimazu

Clan.

It would not be until 1587 that Kyushu would

be conquered by the Hideyoshi Toyotomi and

the Toyotomi Clan as part of their campaign for

unification of all of the islands of Japan.

Invasion of Shikoku

The Invasion of Shikoku occurred in 1585.

It resulted in the Chosokabe Clan surrendering

themselves and the island of Shikoku to the

Toyotomi Clan.

This was significant as the first of the two

islands outside of Honshu would be reunified

with the rest of Japan.

Kyushu Campaign

The Kyushu Campaign occurred in 1587.

It resulted in the Shimazu Clan surrendering

themselves and the island of Kyushu to the

Toyotomi Clan.

This was significant as the second of the two

islands outside of Honshu would be reunified

with the rest of Japan.

The First Anti-Christian Sentiment in Japan

The First Anti-Christian Sentiment occurred in Japan in 1587.

This led to Hideyoshi Toyotomi issuing anti-Christian laws that limited religious activities and ordered foreign missionaries out of the country.

This would be continued under the Tokugawa Shogunate and continue for hundreds of years after the Sengoku Period.

The Siege of Odawara Castle

The Siege of Odawara Castle occurred in 1590.

It resulted in the Toyotmi Clan defeating the

Hojo Clan.

It was similar to the Battle of Appomattox

Court House in the sense that it ended the civil

war under Hideyoshi Toyotomi's rule and led to

reunification of Japan.

Kasai-Osaki Uprising

The Kasai-Osaki Uprising occurred from 1590

to 1591.

This also involved the Kunohe Rebellion as part

of its events.

It led to the Toyotomi Clan defeating the Date

Clan, suppressing riots opposing the Shogunate,

and unifying Japan.

Japan Invades Korea

Japan invaded Korea from 1592 to 1598.

This resulted in China sending an army to

Korea to repel the Japanese.

This led to the Japanese retreating empty-

handed from Korea back to Japan.

Shortly after, Hideyoshi Toyotomi died from

illness, which led to the formation of the

Western Army and Eastern Army in order to

choose a successor for who would be the

Shogun of Japan.

Siege of Otsu Castle

The Siege of Otsu Castle occurred in 1600.

This resulted in the Western Army defeating the

Eastern Army.

It was a part of a series of battles in 1600 that

would eventually lead to the formal end of the

Western Army at the Battle of Sekigahara,

according to the Tokugawa Clan

Siege of Ueda Castle

The Siege of Ueda Castle occurred in 1600.

This resulted in the Sanada Clan defeating the

Tokugawa Clan.

It was a part of a series of battles in 1600 that

would eventually lead to the formal end of the

Western Army at the Battle of Sekigahara,

according to the Tokugawa Clan

Siege of Fushimi Castle

The Siege of Fushimi Castle occurred in 1600.

This resulted in the Western Army defeating the

Eastern Army.

It was a part of a series of battles in 1600 that

would eventually lead to the formal end of the

Western Army at the Battle of Sekigahara,

according to the Tokugawa Clan

Battle of Kusegawa

The Battle of Kusegawa occurred in 1600.

It took place in the Gifu State of the Chubu

Region on the Island of Honshu in Japan.

It was a test of enemy prowess between the

Western Army and the Eastern Army.

It was a part of a series of battles in 1600 that

would eventually lead to the formal end of the

Western Army at the Battle of Sekigahara,

according to the Tokugawa Clan

Siege of Hasedo

The Siege of Hasedo occurred in 1600.

It was fought in the Yamagata state of the

Tohoku Region on the Island of Honshu in

Japan.

It resulted in the Uesugi Clan retreating from

the Date Clan.

It was a part of a series of battles in 1600 that

would eventually lead to the formal end of the

Western Army at the Battle of Sekigahara,

according to the Tokugawa Clan

Battle of Ishigakibaru

The Battle of Ishigakibaru occurred in 1600.

It was primarily fought in the island of Kyushu.

The landscape was very mountainous, making

horseback and ground combat difficult.

It resulted in Western Army surrendering to the

Eastern Army by order of Yoshimune Otomo.

It was a part of a series of battles in 1600 that

would eventually lead to the formal end of the

Western Army at the Battle of Sekigahara,

according to the Tokugawa Clan

The Battle of Sekigahara

The Battle of Sekigahara occurred in 1600.

It was primarily fought in the Gifu State, in the

Chubu Region on the Island of Honshu in

Japan.

Over 42 thousand troops were killed and

another 23 thousand troops defected from the

Western Army to the Eastern Army.

It resulted in the Eastern Army formally

defeating the Western Army.

This would lead to the Tokugawa Clan gaining

nominal control of all of Japan.

Exile of the Sanada Clan

Yukimura Sanada and his father, Masayuki Sanada were exiled to the village of Kudoyama after the Western Army lost the Battle of Sekigahara.

Masayuki Sanada died in exile.

Yukimura Sanada served 14 years in exile before eventually escaping and heading back to join the Western Army in their last standoff against the Eastern Army in 1615 during the Siege of Osaka Castle.

Establishment of the Tokugawa Shogunate

The Tokugawa Shogunate was established in 1603.

It led to Ieyasu Tokugawa being named Shogun of Japan.

As a result, he cracked down on any opposition to his rule and began persecuting foreigners and other western influences, including the Portuguese and the Catholic Church.

The Tokugawa Shogunate lasted from 1603 to 1868.

Catholicism is banned in Japan

Christianity was officially banned in Japan in 1614.

It was done by decree of the Tokugawa Shogunate.

It was mainly done to stop the spread of western influence and meddling in Japanese affairs.

This would eventually lead to the persecution and genocide of Christians in Japan for hundreds of years.

The Siege of Osaka Castle

The Siege of Osaka Castle occurred in 1615.

It was a last-stand battle between the Western

Army and the remaining Toyotomi Loyalists.

It was essentially Japan's version of the Alamo

that resulted in Osaka Castle being burned to

the ground and the Western Army being

defeated and dissolved.

Yukimura Sanada died a warrior's death by

charging alone toward the incoming Tokugawa

Army before being killed by gunfire.

This was the end of the Sengoku Period.

The Shimabara Rebellion

The Shimabara Rebellion occurred in 1638.

It led to the Tokugawa Shogunate strictly

prohibiting Christianity and expelling

Portuguese traders and other western influences

from Japan.

It also led to the persecution of Christians in

Japan.

It was essentially the epilogue to the Sengoku

Period.

Conclusion

Japan's 184 yearlong civil war had a huge impact on its society.

The Tokugawa clan's anti-Catholic sentiment still existed until freedom of religion was allowed in 1889 as a condition to do trade with England.

Unification was eventually achieved after many years of bloodshed over who should succeed Yoshimasa Ashikaga as Shogun of Japan.

Bibliography

Al Jahan, Nabeel. "Tokugawa family and Political system of Edo period."

Birt, Michael P. "Samurai in passage: The transformation of the sixteenth-century Kanto." Journal of Japanese Studies 11.2 (1985).

Butler, Lee. Emperor and Aristocracy in Japan, 1467–1680: Resilience and Renewal. Vol. 209. BRILL, 2020.

Butler, Lee. "The Sixteenth-Century Reunification." Japan Emerging. Routledge, 2018.

Clark, Austin W. "" 100 Spears Worth 100 Pieces": The Impact of Ashigaru on Sengoku Jidai." The Gettysburg Historical Journal 10.1 (2011).

Clement, Ernest Wilson. A short history of Japan. Kyo bun kwan, Christian Literature Society, 1926.

Chen, Lu. "Retelling the History of the Sengoku Period and the Era Name System." biography 43.1 (2020).

Collcutt, Martin C. "Japan in The Muromachi Age." (1978).

Collcutt, Martin. "The Medieval Japanese Daimyo: The Ōuchi Family's Rule of Suō and Nagato." (1981).

Culeddu, Maria Paola. "The Evolution of the Ancient Way of the Warrior: From the Ancient Chronicles to the Tokugawa Period." Asian Studies 6.2 (2018).

Eason, David. "Japan (Sengoku period)." The Encyclopedia of Empire (2016).

Elison, George, and Bardwell L. Smith, eds. Warlords Artists and Commoners: Japan in

the Sixteenth Century. University of
Hawaii Press, 1981.

Fedorova, E. S. "KAMAKURA AND
MUROMACHI PERIODS'MEDICAL
VIEWS IN JAPANESE CULTURE."
Studia Culturae 1.47 (2021).

Gaskin, Carol. *The Ways of the Samurai: From
Ronins to Ninjas, the Fiercest Warriors in
Japan.* Vol. 20120110. 2012.

Gin'ya, Sasaki, and William B. Hauser.
"Sengoku Daimyo Rule and Commerce."
John Whitney Hall, Japan Before

Tokugawa: Political Consolidation and Economic Growth (1981).

Goldman, Eli. "The impact of pikes and guns in Sengoku-Period Japan." (2020).

Hall, John Whitney. "Foundations of the Modern Japanese Daimyo." The Journal of Asian Studies 20.3 (1961).

Hall, S., Nagahara Keiji, and Kozo Yamamura. Japan before Tokugawa: political consolidation and economic growth, 1500-1650. Vol. 704. Princeton University Press, 2014.

Harper, Thomas. "The Kurisaki school of sword wound surgery: From Sengoku to Genroku; Nagasaki to Edo (via Manila)." Uncharted Waters: Intellectual Life in the Edo Period. Brill, 2012.

Haruko, Wakita, and David P. Phillips. "Women and the Creation of the" Ie" in Japan: An Overview from the Medieval Period to the Present." US-Japan Women's Journal. English Supplement 4 (1993).

Henshall, Kenneth. "A History of Japan." From Stone Age to Superpower 2 (2004).

Hisashi, Fujiki, and George Elison. "The political posture of Oda Nobunaga." Japan before Tokugawa: political consolidation and economic growth 1500 (1981).

Keiji, Nagahara. "Medieval Japan. Essays in Institutional History." (1975).

Keiji, Nagahara, and Kozo Yamamura. "Reflections on Recent Trends in Japanese Historiography." Journal of Japanese Studies 10.1 (1984).

Keiji, Nagahara, and Kozo Yamamura. "Shaping the process of unification:

technological progress in sixteenth-and seventeenth-century Japan." Journal of Japanese Studies 14.1 (1988).

Keiji, Nagahara, and Kozo Yamamura. "The Sengoku Daimyo and the Kandaka System." Japan before Tokugawa: Political Consolidation and Economic Growth 1500 (1981).

Keiji, Nagahara, and Kozo Yamamura. "Village Communities and Daimyo Power." CORNELL EAST ASIA SERIES 109 (2001).

Kosaka, Masaaki. "The Meiji Era: the Forces of the Rebirth." Cahiers d'Histoire Mondiale. Journal of World History. Cuadernos de Historia Mundial 5.3 (1960).

Kurashige, Jeff. "The sixteenth century: Identifying a new group of "unifiers" and reevaluating the myth of "reunification"." Routledge Handbook of Premodern Japanese History. Routledge, 2017.

Kurushima, Noriko. "Marriage and female inheritance in medieval Japan."

International Journal of Asian Studies 1.2 (2004).

López-Vera, Jonathan. History of the Samurai: Legendary Warriors of Japan. Tuttle Publishing, 2020.

Lovatt, Joe. Sword and Spirit: Bushido in Practice from the late Sengoku era through the Edo period. Diss. Western Oregon University, 2009.

MAYO, CHRISTOPHER M. "Teaching Premodern Japanese Violence: History and Heritage in the Classroom."

Mcelrath Jr, Iles Kenneth. THE" SEISUISHO"
OF ANRAKUAN SAKUDEN:
HUMOROUS ANECDOTES OF THE
SENGOKU AND EARLY PERIODS.
University of Michigan, 1971.

McKissack, Fraser. "Samurai masculinity,
Japan's self defence force and the uncanny
space–time of Sengoku Jieitai." East Asian
Journal of Popular Culture 3.1 (2017).

Miller, Richard J. "Ancestors and Nobility in
Ancient Japan." World Anthropology
(1976).

Nakamura, James I., and Matao Miyamoto.

"Social structure and population change: A

comparative study of Tokugawa Japan and

Ch'ing China." Economic Development

and Cultural Change 30.2 (1982).

Nelson, David. "The consolidation of place and

punishment in seventeenth-century Japan:

Kanazawa prisons and criminal justice."

Southeast Review of Asian Studies 30

(2008).

Nelson, David G. "Wakita Kyūbei's

Admonitions: A Town Magistrate's

Perspective on Early Modern Warrior Rule." Studies on Asia 4.3 (2013).

Ng, Wai-Ming. "POLITICAL TERMINOLOGY IN THE LEGITIMATION OF THE TOKUGAWA SYSTEM: A STUDY OF" BAKUFU" AND SHŌGUN." Journal of Asian History 34.2 (2000).

Norman, E. Herbert. "Soldier and peasant in Japan: the origins of conscription." Pacific Affairs 16.1 (1943).

Osamu, Wakita. "The emergence of the state in sixteenth-century Japan: from Oda to Tokugawa." Journal of Japanese Studies 8.2 (1982).

Remington, Alexander M. "The Fall of the Ikko Ikki: The Demise of the Honganji in the Late Sengoku Period." (2021).

Richardson, Michael. "TEPPO AND SENGOKU: THE ARQUEBUS IN 16TH CENTURY JAPAN." CONCORD REVIEW (2011).

Saito, Osamu. "The Medieval Origins of

Smithian Growth: The Proliferation of

Occupations and Commodities in Japan,

1261–1638." Social Science Japan Journal

23.2 (2020).

Seyock, Barbara. "Archaeological complexes

from Muromachi period Japan as a

key to the perception of international

maritime trade in East Asia." The East

Asian Mediterranean: Maritime

Crossroads of Culture, Commerce and

Human Migration 6 (2008).

Shamukaev, A., and A. Zakirov. "Evolution of samurai armors of the Sengoku Jidai era." BRIDGE TO SCIENCE: RESEARCH WORKS (2017).

Sheldon, Charles D. "A History of Japan, 1334-1615." (1961).

Shiba, Ryotaro, and Tadashi Hori. "Japanese History: From a Personal Viewpoint." Review of Japanese Culture and Society 1.1 (1986).

Shizuo, Katsumata. "The Development of Sengoku Law." Hall, JW et al.(1981)

Japan Before Tokugawa. Political

Consolidation and Economic Growth 1500

(1981).

Soranaka, Isao. "Hall," et al.", eds.," Japan

before Tokugawa: Political Consolidation

and Economic Growth, 1500-1650"(Book

Review)." Canadian Journal of

History/Annales Canadiennes d'Histoire.

Vol. 16. No. 3. Journal of History Co.,

1981.

Steenstrup, Carl. "The Imagawa Letter: A

Muromachi Warrior's Code of Conduct

Which Became a Tokugawa Schoolbook."
Monumenta Nipponica (1973).

Steinmetz, Suzzane K. "Society and family: A
Brief Overview of the History of Japan."
Japanese Family and Society: Words from
Tongo Takabe, a Meiji Era Sociologist
(2007).

Streich, Philip. "The Failure of the Balance of
Power in Medieval Japan, 1568-1600."
APSA 2009 Toronto Meeting Paper. 2009.

Sugawa-Shimada, Akiko. "'Rekijo' and heritage
tourism: the Sengoku/Bakumatsu boom,

localities and networks." The Theory and Practice of Contents Tourism (2015).

Sugiyama, Shigeki. "Honganji in the Muromachi-Sengoku period: Taking up the sword and its consequences." Pacific World 10 (1994).

Takashi, Yoshida, et al. "The Third Iwanami History Series." (1979).

TANAKA, Tatsuya. "The Settlement Formation of Echigo in the Sengoku Period the Case of Makinome Settlement." Japanese Journal of Human Geography 48.2 (1996).

Tatsuo, Fujita. "The three unifiers of the state (tenka): Nobunaga (1534–82), Hideyoshi (1536–98), and Ieyasu (1543–1616)." The Tokugawa World. Routledge, 2021.

Toyoda, Takeshi. "THE CHARACTER OF THE FEUDAL SOCIETY IN JAPAN (I)." The Annals of the Hitotsubashi Academy 8.1 (1957): 29-35.

Turnbull, Stephen. War in Japan 1467–1615. Bloomsbury Publishing, 2012.

Varley, Paul. "Japan: The Shaping of Daimyo Culture, 1185-1868." (1990).

Varley, Paul. "Warfare in Japan 1467–1600."

War in the early modern world. Routledge,

2005.

WALDMAN, MARILYN R., and HAO

CHANG Columbus. "The Sengoku era in

Japan (sixteenth century) was a crucial

period for." (2003).

Wallace, David. Imperial Significance during

the Formation of Early Modern Japan;

1467-1680. Diss. The Ohio State

University, 2015.

Wilson, George M. "Meiji Ishin: Restoration and Revolution." (1990).

Yamamura, Kozo. "From coins to rice: Hypotheses on the kandaka and kokudaka systems." Journal of Japanese Studies 14.2 (1988).

YAMAZUMI, Hazime. "Village system under the Mori clan regime." Japanese Journal of Human Geography 18.3 (1966).

Yangtai, L. U. "The Analysis of the Characteristics of the karauta of the Samyrai School in the Sengoku Period in

Japan." Contemporary Foreign Languages

Studies 20.1 (2020).